SASS

Erika Verónica Brown

Printed in the U.S.A
ISBN: 978-0-578-81379-0

ACKNOWLEDGMENTS

I would like to take the time to give my thanks to those that directly and indirectly made this book possible.

To my mother, even though she is no longer here, the pride in her voice is a loud and loving encouragement that echoes as I write.

To my children, as they are here not because of a metaphysical accident, but here out of love. I am sorry the planet is not in better shape, as stewards we are failing. But it remains critical that we grasp onto love and grow and embrace life's challenges to find the insight that explains how we are each magical, to reminds us that we are worth caring for, and continue to love tirelessly.

To my dearest husband, the pearl of all pearls, the rock of all rocks, the elm of all elms, and the love of all loves. You are the mountain I lean into; you are the warmth that warms me, and you are the coolest of cats when I need that. Like a silent chameleon, you change your ways without fanfare making everything better, even carrying us to the finishing line if you see us stumble. You make so much room for who I want to be, which gives me pause and say, I take it back, you are not the pearl of all pearls you are what gives them their worth, you are pure luster.

And finally, to my dearest teacher, editor, muse, and friend Pianta, I owe the biggest thanks! You saw this as a book when it was but a lonely poem on a page. Pianta, without you this book would not be a book but a bunch of lost puppies on my desk. Without your editing, they would be shavings for my compost. You gave my poetry a place to be who it is, your class helped me certify myself as a poet, no bigger gift than the permission to be who we are. Pianta, your love for my poetry, your patience with my falta de ortografia, and your wisdom, all mana from the heavens, I am hurrying and cashing it all in before the gods realize all this was not mine to receive, but an address mistake.

I feel so grateful and lucky to have your support.

Thank you.

PREFACE

My inspiration comes from the timbre in the everyday, from the supposition that poetry is in everything and everywhere and the belief that poetry is the portal to all that is divine.

TABLE OF CONTENTS

SUPER SOUL SUNDAY

Sitting under her favorite tree
Oprah
welcomes us into her house
She introduces this week's guest and
invites us to be part of another dimension
another depth
leading us maybe to a new discovery
maybe another truth

In her famous Oprah tone
she poses a question to her guest
what do you know for sure?

The camera focused on her
I am focused on her surroundings; I feel I am there
under her favorite tree
enchanted by all

I don't have a willow tree, but for that moment I do
I don't have majestic grounds
but for that moment I do
I don't have a stone bridge
that rules over a babbling brook
where the quiet moss sways and dances
on unsuspecting rocks, but for that moment I do
I don't have any of the things that Oprah has
but for a moment I do

Pretending to be a guest in Oprah's house, I too can
smell her meadow

I too can feel the drops of morning dew
crunch the carrots from the cornucopia her famous
orchards grow
a bounty so large she shares with all the neighbors, the
kind I don't have, but for that moment I do
I snap back and rewind to that famous question...

Oprah has been asking that same question for over
twenty years now
"What do you know for sure?"
The guest elaborates...
I ask myself that question, again!
This time and after all this time
out of nowhere I scream out loud
I have an answer, Oprah!
I shout out as if she can hear me
and I keep pretending I am the guest and say...

You know what I know for sure Oprah,
I own nothing — nothing!
Not these pearls taken from the sea except for this
moment that they hang on me
nor the diamond heirloom ring
nor the rubies surrounding it
there to remind me
of sweet pomegranate seeds

I own nothing, nothing!
Not the children I call my children, which I brought
forth and so treasure
nor this body I carry around
or better yet
it carries me
not this skin protecting me

whatever the color it is meant to be
no matter how elaborate I ink it to be

No matter what my 401K says
I own nothing
nothing is mine Oprah
I own nothing

I sit here humbled by this truth
no matter how elaborate our surroundings may be
we own nothing
from the beginning to the very end
we own nothing, that

I know for sure

POETRY CLUB NEXT WEDNESDAY

Machinists type up poems
while synapses fire
fireworks that shock our heavy hearts
moments
that remind us to breath
for the eternal unknown reason
that we are here

Live poetry in real-time
zooming in and zooming out
Rachel shows us her dog
Trey, you pet your cat
Sam laughs out loud without any sound
Cam waves a silent hi while a brother sleeps nearby

Like magicians pull rabbits out of hats
we each hide poems in each other's sleeves
others silent but present
all here connecting through our own disconnect
questioning
should the sun even come out tomorrow

For whatever ephemeral reason
poems are the needles we use and share
knitting needles
knitting long poems
knitting seems to be the only thing nudging my sanity
awake

I really could have just stayed in bed
But on Wednesdays
we are all here
waiting for that moment
the moment when the magic happens

when we can taste the sweetness and lightness of the
layered icing on that poetic slice of cake
honored to be served such a bite

Zooming in
and zooming out
we put our poems on the table like poker chips
upping the ante
yet we bet the same for each voice and pronoun
together, like in life, for just a short, yet meaningful
while

Why not turn these earth-shattering moments into an
everlasting memory of effervescence
Let us always come dressed as ourselves
in whatever humanity allows us to share
thus, taking our place to enhance the universe
purposefully, lovingly, soulfully, uniquely
cheering on our shared imperfect humanity
yet celebrating
our poetically perfect existence
See you next Wednesday everybody...

COSTCO SELLS CASKETS

Costco;
our suburban church
we visit Sundays
Wednesdays
Mondays
whenever

I am not a great fan
of Costco's bouncing cacophony
screaming voices through walkie talkies
instructions clearly employees
do not want to hear
much less
me

Am I the only one frazzled
by the church- like vastness
cold refrigerated
areas
cement floors
cathedral ceilings
crates and crates filled to the brim
with god knows what?

Sanctimoniously void of softness
all there to remind us of the power of bulk buying

Costco
the family place where we can buy diabetes in flats
lineup to sample cholesterol on every isle
"America's favorite hot pockets"

People gather around
the all-powerful server, hair net just right

"Two minutes in the microwave and ready to enjoy,
"I hear her say

People, dumb struck,
await flowing baskets parked in disarray
"Stop sampling and get out of the way," I want to scream
but they can't hear me
their brains focused
lost in the free food "zone"

I imagine these families
practicing at home their Costco drills
strategically grabbing as many samples as they can
I want to ask them, "when was the last time you ate?"

My husband doesn't hate Costco;
we joke that this is where he took me to dinner
on our first date
way back when Costco was not even its name

We march in with the faithful
on Sundays, Wednesdays, Mondays
whenever
flashing our elite status with a membership card

The last time we went
the vastness and stadium crowds
overwhelmed me
standing aside
I noticed there were fresh cut flowers in bins
roses and the "variety" bouquet, which
reminded me of the Costco's site

Everything one may need for the BIG day

funeral wreaths and caskets,
"delivered in 3 business days"
"The President," The Royal Silver,"
 and "The Mother's Casket," way too pink for me, but...

Statisticians would say
that my husband is supposed to go first
but the thought of losing him ends the day
life without him unimaginable
losing its entire bulk value

Standing there I see him coming, his arms laden with
all the stuff I like
I smile, god forbid I ran out of Coke Zero and limes

Which again, gives me pause
this time, silently I say, "thanks"
in this churchlike place that we come to
hand in hand on Sundays, Wednesdays, Mondays,
whenever
from the very beginning of us
may it be
till the very end

SWIMMING CAP

In these long dark nights
I swim
never-ending movement
waves just carry me
bobbing up and down in and out
never quite lulling me back to sleep

so I swim
and then I switch sides
I swim on my left side
I swim on my back
I stare at the dark sky
and at some point
I plead and I beg to the gods above

and then
another wave comes
and I turn
maybe the here of the moment
to remind me
I am not in charge

So
I swim
I get cold
I am cold because I took off my socks when I was hot
I keep swimming

It feels darker now
I start thinking
maybe dreaming of that moment
that unbeknownst it just happens
and you fall asleep
only to wake up
and feel beached ashore

like a half dying animal must feel laying on its side
the sun's rays beating down
daring me to wake up

Finally
somehow
my swimming stopped in the middle of the night
land is really where I live best—I hear myself say out
loud

Tonight
no more swimming in the dark
where space and time are a big question in the awake
mind
that place I just left
that place
all insomniacs come to hate

COMPOST

buzzing, chopping, shaving

my shredder has been busy
since I read that I must add "brown" matter to my
compost pile

feeding the grinder drafts of discarded poems
elongated thoughts
now black and white strands
chopped up allusions or broken up illusions
reductions of intentions never quite real visions

just lost-meandering verses
words without any tempo
now compost confetti

worms eating my words
digesting my sighs and filling up on my delirious rants
crunching on remnants of another day just passing by

just another human day
the worms reminded me again
they churn and digest without any trouble
my black and white pearls of wisdom
which are equally delicious
as lint, rotten veggies and dinner leftovers

as I lift the cover
I see most of the rubbish has been turned by the worms
into fine looking soil
Now that, my friends
is organic poetry

DANDELION TEA

Today
I miss my mother

The warmth left for me on this sunny day
waits on the cushion of my favorite chair
sinking in

a blanket of memories enfolds me
and quiets the afternoon

Today
like all days
my mother would have been dressed in her Sunday best
the clock ticking–not on my mother's side
chimes 4 o'clock and breaks my solace
I smile
it is teatime

As her clock announced 4 o'clock
it would always surprise her that time was going by

Invariably she would say, "Oye, ya es la hora del té."
I would jump up into action
instinctively still a fearful and pleasing child
In the kitchen I would preside over the ancient ritual of
putting the kettle to boil
tea leaves full of magic waiting in the pot to turn
boiling water into our favorite kind of wine

As she wiped old crumbs from the table
I would help her straighten the silent eternal tablecloth
lying always flat on his back
our chatter nonstop over the clinking of pairing saucers
with their matching cups

I was never much of a believer of the many "miracles"
my mother bought
nor the need to knit a winter sweater
for the teapot to wear
all the time

Yet, if she were here
or if I was there
we would meet at that place
of warmth comfort and joy
that place
where we both could be our very best

And now, just like at some point in her life
I too miss my mother
pouring plenty of wisdom for me and others

FOOD TO GO

Chicken with mole
Chorizo burrito
Chicken enchilada
Caldo de pollo
Chips and salsa

Death
awaits by his side
back at the house
while we order
Mexican food at the bar

How often do I allow
tequila
sweet and sour mix
jalapeños
salt
seduce me and kiss my lips
make me forget
that death awaits us
back at the house

Back at the house
death with its rattle greets us
the skeleton we left
is thinner
I quickly sober up
my affair with Margarita a memory now

Foil tops keep the fiesta warm
till we sit to eat
Food to go
never looks as good as the pictures the menu promises
will be

Back at house
after dinner mints are not served
but sips of water
and with a dropper
morphine is lovingly given

Unknowingly and in silence
all fighting for the privilege
the honor
to serve the dying
back at the house

Back at the house harmony breaks
egos surface
pettiness commingles with a whiff of decay

We lose our intent

Death can bring out the worst or the best
all in the same day in the very same house
to the very same people
while the dying
keep dying

I pack my ego and huff and puff
so not interested in peacekeeping any more

On my way out
I throw noble intentions in the garbage
that land on the oil pocked bag
full of chips and salsa
none of us ate

back at the house

SASS

did you just say   "I don't get it"

                 is the ink running

is it too   hard   to   read

         you know

      there is no going back

this poem   sassed

      right out of me

     I see you shaking the paper it's on

      are you hoping

      the letters like soldiers

     will get into a different formation

    that makes more sense with your bank of information

I say flick it off like a bugger

         shake it off like dandruff

take Tums   *for the indigestion*

    it may have caused you

                    are you allergic to the type

the gluten   *in the paper*   *DON'T eat it*

        spit it out like hot potato

                spit

    don't   *read*   *reread*

        forcing your brain to try

    to dissect it   *like the eye of the cow*

you did not want to dissect

                            in science class

            it's not a red light

just an intersection   *between*

        "I don't' get it"

                and

it doesn't matter…

You see

a poem is born   *just like cultures*

all magic and mystery

and just like those cultures you don't get

let my poem be

quietly   *walk away*   *leave it*

my poem has no war with you

it won't come after you

it's just   *there*   *existing*

it will be ok

it won't cry alone in the middle of the page
hearing the echo of your footsteps

leaving for now   *unclear*

unchanged

it was not written to your sensibilities

of today

come back another day

some day

Like the first time I encountered Frida Kahlo

I was shocked   disturbed   at the depictions
of violence

my sensibilities   ALL   distraught

but after living nine lives

the two Frida's and I in the same room

now   connect

her blood was her paint

her chest her thick canvas

her pain and agony her muses   peace and love
unattainable

it took nine lives

but now   I   get it

So till then

abort

take the morning after pill   if you have to

whatever

but don't sass my poem

shaking it with salts from different seas

and seasonings from countries

you   have never   even seen

it is under no legal obligation

to be

the light   the beacon

at the end

of your long   or   short tunnel

of vision

ABOUT THE AUTHOR

Erika Verónica Brown is a Certified Medical Spanish Interpreter born in La Paz, Bolivia, to a long line of illustrious poets and writers. Ricardo Jaimes Freyer, her great grand uncle, was the son of the pioneering feminist poet Carolina Freyre Arias de Jaimes, and her husband Julio Lucas Jaimes was famously known by his pen name, "Brocha Gorda."

Brown has read her work at Calit2 Multimedia Theater, at University of California at San Diego, and at Say We All with the Hausmann Quartet. She has participated in the international poster poem exhibitions sponsored by the Canadian Poetry Academy. *SASS* is her second book of poems. Her first, *Momentos*, is a collection of her work in Spanish.

ILLUSTRATION AND DESIGN CREDITS

Metallic background, Сергей Ремизов, Pixabay; Wall texture, Noémie Girardet, Pixabay. Cover design and layout, Pianta.

CURRENT RELEASES

SASS
A chap book of poems
Available on Amazon

Momentos
A collection of original poems in Spanish
Available on Amazon

www.ingramcontent.com/pod-product-compliance
Lightning Source LLC
Chambersburg PA
CBHW071440040426
42445CB00012BA/1402